In the Mountains

Activity Book

Name: _____

Age: _____

Class: _____

School: _____

OXFORD
UNIVERSITY PRESS

Great Clarendon Street, Oxford, OX2 6DP, United Kingdom

Oxford University Press is a department of the University of Oxford.
It furthers the University's objective of excellence in research, scholarship,
and education by publishing worldwide. Oxford is a registered trade
mark of Oxford University Press in the UK and in certain other countries

First published in 2013
2020
10 9 8 7 6 5 4

No unauthorized photocopying

ISBN: 978 0 19 464677 2

Printed in China

This book is printed on paper from certified and well-managed sources

ACKNOWLEDGEMENTS

In the Mountains Activity Book by: Kamini Khanduri

Illustrations by: Kelly Kennedy and Alan Rowe

Introduction ← Page 3

1 Find and write the words.

Coldhotmountainsdrysnowyrivers

1 __cold__   3 _____   5 _____

2 _____   4 _____   6 _____

2 Complete the sentences.

> amazing   ~~mountains~~   dry   rivers

1 Some __mountains__ are cold and snowy.

2 Some mountains are hot and _____.

3 Many big _____ come from mountains.

4 Mountains are _____!

3 Answer the questions.

1 What animals live in the mountains?

_____

2 What can you do in the mountains?

_____

3 Are there mountains where you live?

_____

1 Write the words.

1 h <u>o l e</u>   2 m _____   3 r ____

4 m _____   5 E _____   6 v _____

2 Match. Then write the sentences.

Mountains are   very, very slowly.
Earth's crust moves   high places on Earth.
A volcano is   out of volcanoes.
Hot rock comes   a hole in Earth's crust.

1 _Mountains are high places on Earth._

2 _____

3 _____

4 _____

2 People ← Pages 6–7

1 Write the words.

> grow   transportation   ~~road~~
> electricity   terraces   food

1 ___road___

2 _____

3 _____

4 _____

5 _____

6 _____

2 Order the words.

1 mountains / difficult. / can / be / in the / Living
   <u>Living in the mountains can be difficult.</u>

2 transportation. / for / animals / use / People
   _____

3 Some / don't / electricity. / people / have
   _____

4 homes. / near / grow / People / food / their
   _____

3 Animals ← Pages 8–9

1 Find and write the words.

furalpacapawnestsnowleopardclimb

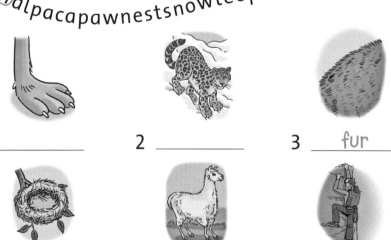

1 _____

2 _____

3 ___fur___

4 _____

5 _____

6 _____

2 Circle the correct words.

1 **Alpacas** / **Golden eagles** make nests on high rocks.

2 Golden eagles have **big** / **small** wings.

3 Snow leopards have big **wings** / **paws**.

4 Snow leopards can **walk** / **fly** on snow.

5 Alpacas have very thick **wings** / **fur**.

6 Alpacas **live** / **don't live** in Asia.

4 Plants ← Pages 10–11

1 Complete the puzzle.

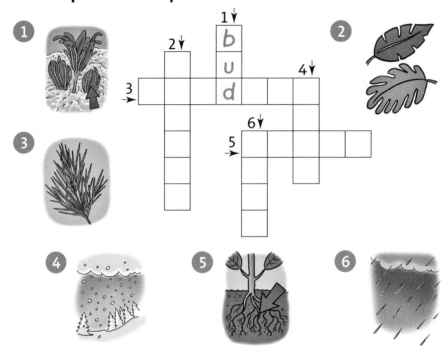

2 Complete the sentences.

long   high   cold   small

1 Conifers have _____ needles.

2 Conifers can grow in _____ places.

3 Some plants can live very _____ in the mountains.

4 Mountain plants have _____ roots.

5 Ice and Snow ← Pages 12–13

1 Write the words.

1 a _ _ _ _ _ _ _ _ _ _   2 d _ _ _ _ _ _ _ _ _ _

3 g _ _ _ _ _ _ _   4 r _ _ _ _ _   5 c _ _ _ _ _ _ _ _

2 Answer the questions.

1 What is a glacier?

A glacier is a river of ice.

2 How do glaciers move?

_____

3 What are crevasses?

_____

4 What is an avalanche?

_____

6 Summer Sports ← Pages 14–15

1 Find and write the words.

a	w	h	e	e	l
s	p	o	r	t	s
h	e	l	m	e	t
o	r	o	p	e	u
f	a	o	s	r	o
u	d	r	a	f	t

1 __rope__

2 _____

3 _____   4 _____   5 _____

2 Write *true* or *false*.

1 Climbers have strong arms and legs. __true__

2 Climbers have a helmet and
  a lifejacket.   _____

3 Climbers find good rocks for their
  hands and feet.   _____

4 Mountain bikes have big,
  strong ropes.   _____

5 Rafting is a great winter sport.   _____

6 Rafts can go over mountains.   _____

1 Write the words. Then match.

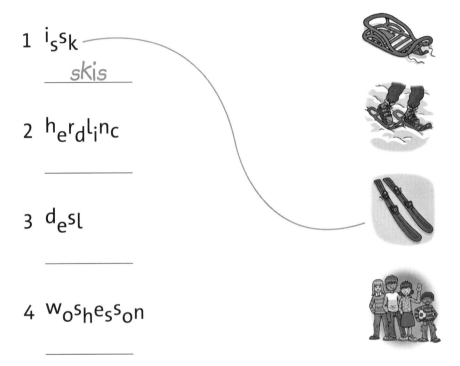

1 i_ss_k

_____skis_____

2 $h_er_dl_inc$

_____

3 d_esl

_____

4 $w_osh_es_on$

_____

2 Circle the correct words.

1 Some children go skiing in the **water** / **mountains**.

2 Snowboarding is a **summer** / **winter** sport.

3 Snowboarders **fall** / **walk** in the snow a lot.

4 **Snowshoes** / **Snowboarders** can do tricks.

5 You **can** / **can't** go fast on a sled.

8 Be Careful! ← Pages 18–19

1 Complete the puzzle. Then write the secret word.

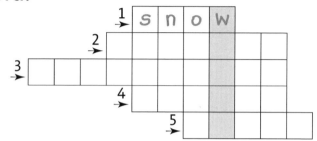

1 → s n o w

2 →

3 →

4 →

5 →

The secret word is:

2 Answer the questions.

1 How are mountains dangerous?

_____

2 What do helicopters do?

_____

3 How is the weather in the mountains?

_____

4 What do you take to the mountains?

_____

After Reading 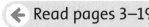 Read pages 3–19

1 Complete the Picture Dictionary.

climb

_____

_____

_____

Earth

_____

_____

_____

_____

_____

_____

_____

_____

_____

ice

_____

_____

_____ _____ mountains _____

_____ _____ _____ _____

 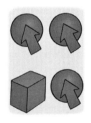  

sports _____ _____ _____

2 Find the words and write the page.

1 You can walk in snowshoes.   __page 17__

2 Crevasses are holes in the ice.   _____

3 They can fly very high.   _____

4 Volcanoes can be dangerous.   _____

5 Some people don't have a car.   _____

6 Don't drink water from a river.   _____

7 Trees can't live there.   _____

8 Climbing is a difficult sport.   _____

3 Write about mountains.

Mountains are _____ places on Earth. Some mountains are cold and some mountains are _____ . Amazing animals _____ in the mountains. Golden eagles can _____ very high. Alpacas have very thick _____ . A river of ice is called a _____ . In summer, people can go _____ in the mountains. In winter, people can go _____ . Have fun in the mountains, but be _____ !

4 Complete the chart.

~~walking~~ ~~river~~ ~~tree~~ snow buds
skiing crevasse rafting roots sledding
avalanche climbing conifer rocks
leaves glacier mountain biking ice
snowboarding needles

In the Mountains	river	_____
	_____	_____
	_____	_____
	_____	
Sports	walking	_____
	_____	_____
	_____	_____
	_____	
Plants	tree	_____
	_____	_____
	_____	

My Book Review

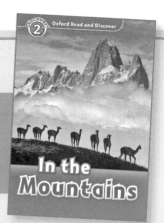

Questions about this book

1 What is this book about?

_____

2 Write six new words from this book.

_____

_____

What I like about this book

My favorite chapter is _____.

My favorite picture is _____.

My favorite new word is _____.

Draw ☺, ☺☺, or ☺☺☺

I like this book. ◯ ◯ ◯

I like the pictures. ◯ ◯ ◯